Roshdy Ebrahim

Countries
Empowerment

By
Roshdy Ebrahim, Ph.D

2020

Roshdy Ebrahim

Roshdy Ebrahim

Contents

Chapter 1

Megacities change the map of the world [1]

I want you to reimagine how life is organized on earth. Think of the planet like a human body that we inhabit. The skeleton is the transportation system of roads and railways, bridges and tunnels, air and seaports that enable our mobility across the continents. The vascular system that powers the body are the oil and gas pipelines and electricity grids. that distribute energy. And the nervous system of communications is the Internet cables, satellites, cellular networks and data centers that allow us to share information.

This ever-expanding infrastructural matrix already consists of 64 million kilometers of roads, four million kilometers of railways, two million kilometers of pipelines and one million kilometers of Internet cables. What about international borders? We have less than 500,000 kilometers of borders.

Let's build a better map of the world. And we can start by overcoming some ancient mythology. There's a saying with which all students of history are familiar: "Geography is destiny." Sounds so grave, doesn't it? It's such a fatalistic adage. It tells us that landlocked

---

[1] parag Khanna: Connectography: Mapping the Future of Global Civilization, amazon, 2016

countries are condemned to be poor, that small countries cannot escape their larger neighbors, that vast distances are insurmountable. But every journey I take around the world, I see an even greater force sweeping the planet: connectivity.

The global connectivity revolution, in all of its forms -- transportation, energy and communications -- has enabled such a quantum leap in the mobility of people, of goods, of resources, of knowledge, such that we can no longer even think of geography as distinct from it. In fact, I view the two forces as fusing together into what I call "connectography."

Connectography represents a quantum leap in the mobility of people, resources and ideas, but it is an evolution, an evolution of the world from political geography, which is how we legally divide the world, to functional geography, which is how we actually use the world, from nations and borders, to infrastructure and supply chains.

Our global system is evolving from the vertically integrated empires of the 19th century, through the horizontally interdependent nations of the 20th century, into a global network civilization in the 21st century. Connectivity, not sovereignty, has become the organizing principle of the human species.

We are becoming this global network civilization because we are literally building it. All of the world's defense budgets and military spending taken together total just under two trillion dollars per year. Meanwhile, our global infrastructure spending is projected to rise to nine trillion dollars per year within the coming decade. And, well, it should. We have been living off an infrastructure stock meant for a world population of three billion, as our population has crossed seven billion to eight billion and eventually nine billion and more. As a rule of thumb, we should spend about one trillion dollars on the basic infrastructure needs of every billion people in the world.

Not surprisingly, Asia is in the lead. In 2015, China announced the creation of the Asian Infrastructure Investment Bank, which together with a network of other organizations aims to construct a network of iron and silk roads, stretching from Shanghai to Lisbon.

And as all of this topographical engineering unfolds, we will likely spend more on infrastructure in the next 40 years, we will build more infrastructure in the next 40 years, than we have in the past 4,000 years.

Now let's stop and think about it for a minute. Spending so much more on building the foundations of global society rather than on the tools to destroy it can have profound consequences. Connectivity is how we optimize the distribution of people and resources around the world. It is how mankind comes to be more than just the sum of its parts. I believe that is what is happening.

Connectivity has a twin megatrend in the 21st century: planetary urbanization. Cities are the infrastructures that most define us. By 2030, more than two thirds of the world's population will live in cities. And these are not mere little dots on the map, but they are vast archipelagos stretching hundreds of kilometers.

Here we are in Vancouver, at the head of the Cascadia Corridor that stretches south across the US border to Seattle. The technology powerhouse of Silicon Valley begins north of San Francisco down to San Jose and across the bay to Oakland. The sprawl of Los Angeles now passes San Diego across the Mexican border to Tijuana. San Diego and Tijuana now share an airport terminal where you can exit into either country. Eventually, a high-speed rail network may connect the entire Pacific spine. America's northeastern megalopolis begins in Boston through New York and Philadelphia to Washington. It contains more than 50 million people and also has plans for a high-speed rail network.

But Asia is where we really see the megacities coming together. This continuous strip of light from Tokyo through Nagoya to Osaka contains more than 80 million people and most of Japan's economy. It is the world's largest megacity. For now.

But in China, megacity clusters are coming together with populations reaching 100 million people. The Bohai Rim around Beijing, The Yangtze River Delta around Shanghai and the Pearl River Delta, stretching from Hong Kong north to Guangzhou. And in the middle, the Chongqing-Chengdu megacity cluster, whose geographic footprint is almost the same size as the country of Austria.

And any number of these megacity clusters has a GDP approaching two trillion dollars -- that's almost the same as all of India today. So imagine if our global diplomatic institutions, such as the G20, were to base their membership on economic size rather than national representation. Some Chinese megacities may be in and have a seat at the table, while entire countries, like Argentina or Indonesia would be out.

Moving to India, whose population will soon exceed that of China, it too has a number of megacity clusters, such as the Delhi Capital Region and Mumbai. In the Middle East, Greater Tehran is absorbing one third of Iran's population. Most of Egypt's 80 million people live in the corridor between Cairo and Alexandria. And in the gulf, a necklace of city-states is forming, from Bahrain and Qatar, through the United Arab Emirates to Muscat in Oman.

And then there's Lagos, Africa's largest city and Nigeria's commercial hub. It has plans for a rail network that will make it the anchor of a vast Atlantic coastal corridor, stretching across Benin, Togo and Ghana, to Abidjan, the capital of the Ivory Coast.

But these countries are suburbs of Lagos. In a megacity world, countries can be suburbs of cities. By 2030, we will have as many as 50 such megacity clusters in the world. So which map tells you more? Our traditional map of 200 discrete nations that hang on most of our walls, or this map of the 50 megacity clusters?

And yet, even this is incomplete because you cannot understand any individual megacity without understanding its connections to the others. People move to cities to be connected, and connectivity is why these cities thrive. Any number of them, such as Sao Paulo or Istanbul or Moscow, has a GDP approaching or exceeding one third of one half of their entire national GDP.

But equally importantly, you cannot calculate any of their individual value without understanding the role of the flows of people, of finance, of technology that enable them to thrive. Take the Gauteng province of South Africa, which contains Johannesburg and the capital Pretoria. It too represents just over a third of South Africa's GDP. But equally importantly, it is home to the offices of almost every single multinational corporation that invests directly into South Africa and indeed, into the entire African continent.

Cities want to be part of global value chains. They want to be part of this global division of labor. That is how cities think. I've never met a mayor who said to me, "I want my city to be cut off." They know that their cities belong as much to the global network civilization as to their home countries.

Now, for many people, urbanization causes great dismay. They think cities are wrecking the planet. But right now, there are more than 200 intercity learning networks thriving. That is as many as the number of intergovernmental organizations that we have. And all of these intercity networks are devoted to one purpose, mankind's number one priority in the 21st century: sustainable urbanization.

Is it working? Let's take climate change. We know that summit after summit in New York and Paris is not going to reduce greenhouse gas emissions. But what we can see is that transferring technology and knowledge and policies between cities is how we've actually begun to reduce the carbon intensity of our economies.

Cities are learning from each other. How to install zero-emissions buildings, how to deploy electric car-sharing systems. In major Chinese cities, they're imposing quotas on the number of cars on the streets. In many Western cities, young people don't even want to drive anymore. Cities have been part of the problem, now they are part of the solution.

Inequality is the other great challenge to achieving sustainable urbanization. When I travel through megacities from end to end -- it takes hours and days -- I experience the tragedy of extreme disparity within the same geography. And yet, our global stock of financial assets has never been larger, approaching 300 trillion dollars. That's almost four times the actual GDP of the world.

We have taken on such enormous debts since the financial crisis, but have we invested them in inclusive growth? No, not yet. Only when we build sufficient, affordable public housing, when we invest in robust transportation networks to allow people to connect to each other both physically and digitally, that's when our divided cities and societies will come to feel whole again.

And that is why infrastructure has just been included in the United Nations Sustainable Development Goals, because it enables all the others. Our political and economic leaders are learning that connectivity is not charity, it's opportunity. And that's why our financial community needs to understand that connectivity is the most important asset class of the 21st century.

Now, cities can make the world more sustainable, they can make the world more equitable, I also believe that connectivity between cities can make the world more peaceful. If we look at regions of the world with dense relations across borders, we see more trade, more investment and more stability. We all know the story of Europe after World War II, where industrial integration kicked off a process that gave rise to today's peaceful European Union. And you can see that Russia, by the way, is the least connected of major powers in the international system. And that goes a long way towards explaining the tensions today. Countries that have less stake in the system also have less to lose in disturbing it. In North America, the lines that matter most on the map are not the US-Canada border or the US-Mexico border, but the dense network of roads and railways and pipelines and electricity grids and even water canals that are forming an integrated North American union. North America does not need more walls, it needs more connections.

But the real promise of connectivity is in the postcolonial world. All of those regions where borders have historically been the most arbitrary and where generations of leaders have had hostile relations with each other. But now a new group of leaders has come into power and is burying the hatchet.

Let's take Southeast Asia, where high-speed rail networks are planned to connect Bangkok to Singapore and trade corridors from Vietnam to Myanmar. Now this region of 600 million people coordinates its agricultural resources and its industrial output. It is evolving into what I call a Pax Asiana, a peace among Southeast Asian nations.

A similar phenomenon is underway in East Africa, where a half dozen countries are investing in railways and multimodal corridors so that landlocked countries can get their goods to market. Now these countries coordinate their utilities and their investment policies. They, too, are evolving into a Pax Africana.

One region we know could especially use this kind of thinking is the Middle East. As Arab states tragically collapse, what is left behind but the ancient cities, such as Cairo, Beirut and Baghdad? In fact, the nearly 400 million people of the Arab world are almost entirely urbanized. As societies, as cities, they are either water rich or water poor, energy rich or energy poor. And the only way to correct these mismatches is not through more wars and more borders, but through more connectivity of pipelines and water canals. Sadly, this is not yet the map of the Middle East. But it should be, a connected Pax Arabia, internally integrated and productively connected to its neighbors: Europe, Asia and Africa.

Now, it may not seem like connectivity is what we want right now towards the world's most turbulent region. But we know from history that more connectivity is the only way to bring about stability in the long run. Because we know that in region after region, connectivity is the new reality. Cities and countries are learning to aggregate into more peaceful and prosperous wholes.

But the real test is going to be Asia. Can connectivity overcome the patterns of rivalry among the great powers of the Far East? After all, this is where World War III is supposed to break out. Since the end of the Cold War, a quarter century ago, at least six major wars have been predicted for this region. But none have broken out.

Take China and Taiwan. In the 1990s, this was everyone's leading World War III scenario. But since that time, the trade and investment volumes across the straits have become so intense that last November, leaders from both sides held a historic summit to discuss eventual peaceful reunification. And even the election of a nationalist party in Taiwan that's pro-independence earlier this year does not undermine this fundamental dynamic.

China and Japan have an even longer history of rivalry and have been deploying their air forces and navies to show their strength in island disputes. But in recent years, Japan has been making its largest foreign investments in China. Japanese cars are selling in record numbers there. And guess where the largest number of foreigners residing in Japan today comes from? You guessed it: China.

China and India have fought a major war and have three outstanding border disputes, but today India is the second largest shareholder in the Asian Infrastructure Investment Bank. They're building a trade corridor stretching from Northeast India through Myanmar and Bangladesh to Southern China. Their trade volume has grown from 20 billion dollars a decade ago to 80 billion dollars today.

Nuclear-armed India and Pakistan have fought three wars and continue to dispute Kashmir, but they're also negotiating a most-favored-nation trade agreement and want to complete a pipeline stretching from Iran through Pakistan to India.

And let's talk about Iran. Wasn't it just two years ago that war with Iran seemed inevitable? Then why is every single major power rushing to do business there today?

Ladies and gentlemen, I cannot guarantee that World War III will not break out. But we can definitely see why it hasn't happened yet. Even though Asia is home to the world's fastest growing militaries, these same countries are also investing billions of dollars in each other's infrastructure and supply chains. They are more interested in each other's functional geography than in their political geography. And that is why their leaders think twice, step back from the brink, and decide to focus on economic ties over territorial tensions.

So often it seems like the world is falling apart, but building more connectivity is how we put Humpty Dumpty back together again, much better than before. And by wrapping the world in such seamless physical and digital connectivity, we evolve towards a world in which people can rise above their geographic constraints. We are the cells and vessels pulsing through these global connectivity networks.

Every day, hundreds of millions of people go online and work with people they've never met. More than one billion people cross borders every year, and that's expected to rise to three billion in the coming decade.

We don't just build connectivity, we embody it. We are the global network civilization, and this is our map. A map of the world in which geography is no longer destiny. Instead, the future has a new and more hopeful motto: connectivity is destiny.

Chapter 2

Cities rule the world [1]

Cities are the 21st century's dominant form of civilization — and they're where humanity's struggle for survival will take place.

Half the planet's population lives in cities. They are the world's engines, generating four-fifths of the global GDP. There are over 2,100 cities with populations of 250,000 people or more, including a growing number of mega-cities and sprawling, networked-city areas — conurbations, they're called — with at least 10 million residents. As the economist Ed Glaeser puts it, "we are an urban species."

But what makes cities so incredibly important is not just population or economics stats. Cities are humanity's most realistic hope for future democracy to thrive, from the grassroots to the global. This makes them a stark contrast to so many of today's nations, increasingly paralyzed by polarization, corruption and scandal.

Cities are a promising alternative for fostering effective and pragmatic democracy from the ground up

---

)¹ ***Robert Muggah***: *research director of the Igarapé Institute and the SecDev Foundation. **Benjamin Barber**: a political theorist and the founder of the Global Parliament of Mayors.*

National dysfunction is hardly restricted to Congressional gridlock in the United States and the dark carnival of the Presidential primaries. It is also rife in Brazil where an elected President was impeached by a national congress, over 50 percent of whose members face criminal investigations. From Hungary to Poland, angry, right-wing populist administrations are taking charge. In the Philippines, a hard-boiled gunslinger has assumed the presidency. The countries of the Arab Spring have become engulfed in vicious wars, terrorist insurrections and junta governments.

Against this grim backdrop, cities are a promising alternative for democracy to thrive naturally. Where nations are independent, competitive and defined by rigid borders, cities are cooperative, made for trade and defined by bridges rather than borders. And increasingly, cities are getting connected and becoming the most interdependent of political entities.

Large and medium-sized cities — especially in North America and Western Europe — have forged networks between and within national boundaries. Linked together by exchanges of ideas, capital and people, and facing common challenges like climate change, inequality and terrorism, intercity networks are a kind of new normal.

Not all cities are equally connected, though. Some of the world's 30-odd mega-cities are linked together in clusters of culture, commerce, labor and infrastructure. Hundreds of large cities are connecting to an international urban grid; thousands more aspire to connectivity. In order for "glocal" urban relationships to succeed, cities will need to squarely address the inequality that allows some cities to prosper while leaving many others behind.

There are hundreds, even thousands, of fast-growing cities in Africa, Asia and the Americas that are literally and figuratively off the grid. Glamorous cities of the future — London, New York, Paris, Shanghai and Singapore — are diverting our gaze from southerly cities where the vast majority of future population growth will take place.

Many of these cities — most with names you've never heard of — are struggling to attract investment, enduring gut-wrenching levels of crime and violence and suffering from extreme inequality and grinding poverty, along the lines of what urban theorist Mike Davis described in his book *Planet of Slums*. As successful cities come together to weave a better, stronger future, these "fragile cities" watch helplessly as their urban fabric unravels.

What is missing is a global governance body constructed purposefully for and by cities

One way to help cities of all kinds benefit from the urban revolution is to build new avenues of intercity and cross-border collaboration. The last few decades witnessed an explosion of city networks, many of them focusing on specific problems. The United Cities and Local Government (UCLG) is one of the better-known alliances. Established just over a decade ago, it claims to advocate on behalf of 240,000 towns, cities and metropolises from 140 countries.

In the area of public security, there is the European Forum and Urban Security (EFUS) and the newly established Strong Cities network. For better housing and environmental protection, there is the International Clearing House on Sustainable Development and Environmental Protection (ICELI) which works with over 1,000 cities and towns to build more livable cities. In the realm of climate change, there is the C40 Climate Cities network, a group composed of 80 cities founded ten years ago by three mayors (London's Ken Livingstone, Toronto's David Miller and New York's Michael Bloomberg).

While this burst of city networking is remarkable, it's not enough. What's missing is a global governance body constructed purposefully for and by cities. The Global Parliament of Mayors — the first gathering of which will occur in The Hague between September 10 and 12 this year — is a step in that direction. The GPM is not just an abstract idea; it's a real expression of city-driven collective action. And it may prove a nimble and potent force in an era where existing structures — like the United Nations General Assembly or Security Council — are not up to addressing our most dire global threats.

The road ahead is pocked — cratered even — with uncertainty. There are no simple solutions to our planet's most pressing problems. What is clear, though, is that the struggle for justice, equality and sustainable growth will take place in cities — and that any true success has to include the cities and citizens of the Global South. Many of the most ingenious and effective responses come from cities with intractable problems, and the fact that cities and urban residents are rolling up their sleeves and getting things done — where nations have failed — offers real grounds for hope.

In the future, it may not be so much senators, governors and or even heads of state that will define our fates — but mayors. Let's make sure they have all the tools at their disposal to succeed.

Chapter 3

Risks facing cities [1]

Cities are the most extraordinary experiment in social engineering that we humans have ever come up with. If you live in a city, and even if you live in a slum -- which 20 percent of the world's urban population does -- you're likely to be healthier, wealthier, better educated and live longer than your country cousins. There's a reason why three million people are moving to cities every single week. Cities are where the future happens first. They're open, they're creative, they're dynamic, they're democratic, they're cosmopolitan, they're sexy. They're the perfect antidote to reactionary nationalism. But cities have a dark side. They take up just three percent of the world's surface area, but they account for more than 75 percent of our energy consumption, and they emit 80 percent of our greenhouse gases. There are hundreds of thousands of people who die in our cities every single year from violence, and millions more who are killed as a result of car accidents and pollution. In Brazil, where I live, we've got 25 of the 50 most homicidal cities on the planet. And a quarter of our cities have chronic water shortages -- and this, in a country with 20 percent of the known water reserves.

)[1] Robert Muggah: megacities expert.

So, cities are dual-edged. Part of the problem is that, apart from a handful of megacities in the West and the Far East, we don't know that much about the thousands of cities in Africa, in Latin America, in Asia, where 90 percent of all future population growth is set to take place. So why this knowledge gap? Well, part of the problem is that we still see the world through the lens of nation-states. We're still locked in a 17th-century paradigm of parochial national sovereignty. And yet, in the 1600's, when nation-states were really coming into their own, less than one percent of the world's population resided in a city. Today, it's 54 percent. And by 2050, it will be closer to 70 percent. So, the world has changed. We have these 193 nation-states, but we have easily as many cities that are beginning to rival them in power and influence.

Just look at New York. The Big Apple has 8.5 million people and an annual budget of 80 billion dollars. Its GDP is 1.5 trillion, which puts it higher than Argentina and Australia, Nigeria and South Africa. Its roughly 40,000 police officers mean it has one of the largest police departments in the world, rivaling all but the largest nation-states. But cities like New York or São Paulo or Johannesburg or Dhaka or Shanghai -- they're punching above their weight economically, but below their weight politically. And that's going to have to change. Cities are going to have to find their political voice if we want to change things.

Now, I want to talk to you a little bit about the risks that cities are facing -- some of the big mega-risks. I'm also going to talk to you briefly about some of the solutions. I'm going to do this using a big data visualization that was developed with Carnegie Mellon's CREATE Lab and my institute, along with many, many others. I want you to first imagine the world not as made up of nation-states, but as made up of cities. What you see here is every single city with a population of a quarter million people or more. Now, without going into technical detail, the redder the circle, the more fragile that city is, and the bluer the circle, the more resilient. Fragility occurs when the social contract comes unstuck. And what we tend to see is a convergence of multiple kinds of risks: income inequality, poverty, youth unemployment, different issues around violence, even exposure to droughts, cyclones and earthquakes. Now obviously, some cities are more fragile than others.

The good news, if there is any, is that fragility is not a permanent condition. Some cities that were once the most fragile cities in the world, like Bogotá in Colombia or Ciudad Juárez in Mexico, have now fallen more around the national average. The bad news is that fragility is deepening, especially in those parts of the world that are most vulnerable, in North Africa, the Middle East, in South Asia and

Central Asia. There, we're seeing fragility rising way beyond scales we've ever seen before. When cities become too fragile, they can collapse, tip over and fail. And when that happens, we have explosive forms of migration: refugees.

There are more than 22 million refugees in the world today, more than at any other time since the second world war. Now, there's not one refugee crisis; there are multiple refugee crises. And contrary to what you might read in the news, the vast majority of refugees aren't fleeing from poor countries to wealthy countries, they're moving from poor cities into even poorer cities -- often, cities nearby. Every single dot on this map represents an agonizing story of struggle and survival. But I want to briefly tell you about what's not on that map, and that's internal displacement. There are more than 36 million people who have been internally displaced around the world. These are people living in refugee-like conditions, but lacking the equivalent international protection and assistance. And to understand their plight, I want to zoom in briefly on Syria.

Syria suffered one of the worst droughts in its history between 2007 and 2010. More than 75 percent of its agriculture and 85 percent of its livestock were wiped out. And in the process, over a million people moved into cities like Aleppo, Damascus and Homs. As food prices began to rise, you also had equivalent levels of social unrest. And when the regime of President Assad began cracking down, you had an explosion of refugees. You also had over six million internally displaced people, many of whom when on to become refugees. And they didn't just move to neighboring countries like Jordan or Lebanon or Turkey. They also moved up north towards Western Europe. See, over 1.4 million Syrians made the perilous journey through the Mediterranean and up through Turkey to find their way into two countries, primarily: Germany and Sweden.

Now, climate change -- not just drought, but also sea level rise, is probably one of the most severe existential threats that cities face. That's because two-thirds of the world's cities are coastal. Over 1.5 billion people live in low-lying, flood-prone coastal areas. What you see here is a map that shows sea level rise in relation to changes in temperature. Climate scientists predict that we're going to see anywhere between three and 30 feet of sea level rise this side of the century. And it's not just low island nation-states that are going to suffer -- Kiribati or the Maldives or the Solomons or Sri Lanka -- and they will suffer, but also massive cities like Dhaka, like Hong Kong, like Shanghai. Cities of 10, 20, 30 million people or more are literally going to be wiped off the face of this earth. They're going to have to adapt, or they're going to die.

I want to take you also all the way over to the West, because this isn't just a problem in

Asia or Africa or Latin America, this is a problem also in the West. This is Miami. Many of you know Miami is one of the wealthiest cities in the United States; it's also one of the most flood-prone. That's been made painfully evident by natural disasters throughout 2017. But Miami is built on porous limestone -- a swamp. There's no way any kind of flood barrier is going to keep the water from seeping in. As we scroll back, and we look across the Caribbean and along the Gulf, we begin to realize that those cities that have suffered worst from natural crises -- Port-au-Prince, New Orleans, Houston -- as severe and as awful as those situations have been, they're a dress rehearsal for what's to come.

No city is an island. Every city is connected to its rural hinterland in complex ways -- often, in relation to the production of food. I want to take you to the northern part of the Amazon, in Rondônia. This is one of the world's largest terrestrial carbon sinks, processing millions of carbons every single year. What you see here is a single road over a 30-year period. On either side you see land being cleared for pasture, for cattle, but also for soy and sugar production. You're seeing deforestation on a massive scale. The red area here implies a net loss of forest over the last 14 years. The blue, if you could see it -- there's not much -- implies there's been an incremental gain. Now, as grim and gloomy as the situation is -- and it is -- there is a little bit of hope.

the Brazilian government, from the national to the state to the municipal level, has also introduced a whole range -- a lattice -- of parks and protected areas. And while not perfect, and not always limiting encroachment, they have served to tamp back deforestation. The same applies not just in Brazil but all across the Americas, into the United States, Canada and around the world. So, let's talk about solutions. Despite climate denial at the highest levels, cities are taking action. You know, when the US pulled out of the Paris Climate Agreement, hundreds of cities in the United States and thousands more around the world doubled down on their climate commitments.

And when the White House cracked down on so-called "undocumented migrants" in sanctuary cities, hundreds of cities and counties and states sat up in defiance and refused to enact that order.

But we're going to need to see a lot more of it, especially in the global south. You see, parts of Africa and Latin America are urbanizing before they industrialize. They're growing at three times the global average in terms their population. And this is putting enormous strain on infrastructure and services. Now, there is a golden opportunity. It's a small opportunity but a golden one: in the next 10 to 20 years, to really start designing in principles of resilience into our cities. There's not one single way of doing this, but there are a number of ways that are emerging. And I've spoken with hundreds of urban planners, development specialists, architects and civic activists, and a number of recurring principles keep coming out. I just want to pass on six.

First: cities need a plan and a strategy to implement it. I mean, it sounds crazy, but the vast majority of world cities don't actually have a plan or a vision. They're too busy putting out daily fires to think ahead strategically. I mean, every city wants to be creative, happy, liveable, resilient -- who doesn't? The challenge is, how do you get there? And urban governance plays a key role. You could do worse than take a page from the book of Singapore. In 1971, Singapore set a 50-year urban strategy and renews it every five years. What Singapore teaches us is not just the importance of continuity, but also the critical role of autonomy and discretion. Cities need the power to be able to issue debt, to raise taxes, to zone effectively, to build affordable housing. What cities need is nothing less than a devolution revolution, and this is going to require renegotiating the terms of the contract with a nation-state.

Second: you've got to go green. Cities are already leading global decarbonization efforts. They're investing in congestion pricing schemes, in climate reduction emission targets, in biodiversity, in parks and bikeways and walkways and everything in between. There's an extraordinary menu of options they have to choose from. One of the great things is, cities are already investing heavily in renewables -- in solar and wind -- not just in North America, but especially in Western Europe and parts of Asia. There are more than 8,000 cities right now in the world today with solar plants. There are 300 cities that have declared complete energy autonomy. One of my favorite stories comes from Medellín, which invested in a municipal hydroelectric plant, which doesn't only service its local needs, but allows the city to sell excess energy back onto the national grid. And it's not alone. There are a thousand other cities just like it.

Third: invest in integrated and multi-use solutions. The most successful cities are those that are going to invest in solutions that don't solve just one problem, but that solve multiple problems. Take the case of integrated public transport. When done well -- rapid bus transit, light rail, bikeways, walkways, boatways -- these can dramatically reduce emissions and congestion. But they can do a lot more than that. They can improve public health. They can reduce dispersion. They can even increase safety. A great example of this comes from Seoul. You see, Seoul's population doubled over the last 30 years, but the footprint barely changed. How? Well, 75 percent of Seoul's residents get to work using what's been described as one of the most extraordinary public transport systems in the world. And Seoul used to be car country.

Next, fourth: build densely but also sustainably. The death of all cities is the sprawl. Cities need to know how to build resiliently, but also in a way that's inclusive. This is a picture right here of Dallas-Fort Worth. And what you see is its population also doubled over the last 30 years. But as you can see, it spread into edge cities and suburbia as far as the eye can see. Cities need to know when not to build, so as not to reproduce urban sprawl and slums of downward accountability. The problem with Dallas-Forth Worth is just five percent of its residents get to work using public transport -- five. Ninety-five percent use cars, which partly explains why it's got some of the longest commuting times in North America. Singapore, by contrast, got it right. They built vertically and built in affordable housing to boot.

Fifth: steal. The smartest cities are nicking, pilfering, stealing, left, right and center. They don't have time to waste. They need tomorrow's technology today, and they're going to leapfrog to get there. This is New York, but it's not just New York that's doing a lot of stealing, it's Singapore, it's Seoul, it's Medellín. The urban renaissance is only going to be enabled when cities start borrowing from one another.

And finally: work in global coalitions. You know, there are more than 200 inner-city coalitions in the world today. There are more city coalitions than there are coalitions for nation-states. Just take a look at the Global Parliament of Mayors, set up by the late Ben Barber, who was driving an urban rights movement. Or consider the C40, a marvelous network of cities that has gathered thousands together to deliver clean energy. Or look at the World Economic Forum, which is developing smart city protocols. Or the 100 Resilient Cities initiative, which is leading a resilience revival. ICLEI, UCLG, Metropolis -- these are the movements of the future. What they all realize is that when cities work together, they can amplify their voice, not just on the national stage, but on the global stage. And with a voice comes, potentially, a vote -- and then maybe even a veto.

When nation-states default on their national sovereignty, cities have to step up. They can't wait. And they don't need to ask for permission. They can exert their own sovereignty. They understand that the local and the global have really, truly come together, that we live in a global, local world, and we need to adjust our politics accordingly. As I travel around the world and meet mayors and civic leaders, I'm amazed by the energy, enthusiasm and effectiveness they bring to their work. They're pragmatists. They're problem-solvers. They're para-diplomats. And in this moment of extraordinary international uncertainty, when our multilateral institutions are paralyzed and our nation-states are in retreat, cities and their leaders are our new 21st-century visionaries. They deserve -- no, they have a right to -- a seat at the table.

Chapter 4

Civilization could destroy itself [1]

It's trying to think about a sort of structural feature of the current human condition. You like the urn metaphor, so I'm going to use that to explain it. So, picture a big urn filled with balls representing ideas, methods, possible technologies. You can think of the history of human creativity as the process of reaching into this urn and pulling out one ball after another, and the net effect so far has been hugely beneficial, right? We've extracted a great many white balls, some various shades of gray, mixed blessings. We haven't so far pulled out the black ball -- a technology that invariably destroys the civilization that discovers it. So, the paper tries to think about what could such a black ball be.

I guess it's just meant to illustrate the difficulty of foreseeing what basic discoveries will lead to. We just don't have that capability. Because we have become quite good at pulling out balls, but we don't really have the ability to put the ball back into the urn, right. We can invent, but we can't un-invent. So, our strategy, such as it is, is to hope that there is no black ball in the urn.

So, the easiest type to understand is a technology that just makes it very easy to cause

---

)[1] Nick Bostrom: philosopher.

massive amounts of destruction. Synthetic biology might be a fecund source of that kind of black ball, but many other possible things we could -- think of geoengineering, really great, right? We could combat global warming, but you don't want it to get too easy either, you don't want any random person and his grandmother to have the ability to radically alter the earth's climate. Or maybe lethal autonomous drones, massed-produced, mosquito-sized killer bot swarms. Nanotechnology, artificial general intelligence.

so think back to the 1930s where for the first time we make some breakthroughs in nuclear physics, some genius figures out that it's possible to create a nuclear chain reaction and then realizes that this could lead to the bomb. And we do some more work, it turns out that what you require to make a nuclear bomb is highly enriched uranium or plutonium, which are very difficult materials to get. You need ultracentrifuges, you need reactors, like, massive amounts of energy. But suppose it had turned out instead there had been an easy way to unlock the energy of the atom. That maybe by baking sand in the microwave oven or something like that you could have created a nuclear detonation. So we know that that's physically impossible. But before you did the relevant physics how could you have known how it would turn out?

unless there were something that is easy to do on purpose but that wouldn't happen by random chance. So, like things we can easily do, we can stack 10 blocks on top of one another, but in nature, you're not going to find, like, a stack of 10 blocks.

so think about what that would have meant if, say, anybody by working in their kitchen for an afternoon could destroy a city. It's hard to see how modern civilization as we know it could have survived that. Because in any population of a million people, there will always be some who would, for whatever reason, choose to use that destructive power. So if that apocalyptic residual would choose to destroy a city, or worse, then cities would get destroyed.

so in addition to these kind of obvious types of black balls that would just make it possible to blow up a lot of things, other types would act by creating bad incentives for humans to do things that are harmful. So, the Type-2a, we might call it that, is to think about some technology that incentivizes great powers to use their massive amounts of force to create destruction. So, nuclear weapons were actually very close to this, right? What we did, we spent over 10 trillion dollars to build 70,000 nuclear warheads and put them on hair-trigger alert. And there were several times during the Cold War we almost blew each other up. It's not because a lot of people felt this would be a great idea, let's all spend 10 trillion dollars to blow ourselves up, but the incentives were such that we were finding ourselves -- this could have been worse. Imagine if there had been a safe first strike. Then it might have been very tricky, in a crisis situation, to refrain from launching all their nuclear missiles. If nothing else, because you would fear that the other side might do it.

It could have been more unstable than it was. And there could be other properties of technology. It could have been harder to have arms treaties, if instead of nuclear weapons there had been some smaller thing or something less distinctive.

so, here we might take the case of global warming. There are a lot of little conveniences that cause each one of us to do things that individually have no significant effect, right? But if billions of people do it, cumulatively, it has a damaging effect. Now, global warming could have been a lot worse than it is. So we have the climate sensitivity parameter, right. It's a parameter that says how much warmer does it get if you emit a certain amount of greenhouse gases. But, suppose that it had been the case that with the amount of greenhouse gases we emitted, instead of the temperature rising by, say, between three and 4.5 degrees by 2100, suppose it had been 15 degrees or 20 degrees. Like, then we might have been in a very bad situation. Or suppose that renewable energy had just been a lot harder to do. Or that there had been more fossil fuels in the ground.

You could imagine other features. So, right now, it's a little bit difficult to switch to renewables and stuff, right, but it can be done. But it might just have been, with slightly different physics, it could have been much more expensive to do these things.

I think there might well be various black balls in the urn, that's what it looks like. There might also be some golden balls that would help us protect against black balls. And I don't know which order they will come out.

if we just keep inventing, like, eventually we will pull out all the balls. I mean, I think there's a kind of weak form of technological determinism that is quite plausible, like, you're unlikely to encounter a society that uses flint axes and jet planes. But you can almost think of a technology as a set of affordances. So technology is the thing that enables us to do various things and achieve various effects in the world. How we'd then use that, of course depends on human choice. But if we think about these three types of vulnerability, they make quite weak assumptions about how we would choose to use them. So a Type-1 vulnerability, again, this massive, destructive power, it's a fairly weak assumption to think that in a population of millions of people there would be some that would choose to use it destructively.

I think, we get more and more power, and [it's] easier and easier to use those powers, but we can also invent technologies that kind of help us control how people use those powers.

Restricting technological development doesn't seem promising, if we are talking about a general halt to technological progress. I think neither feasible, nor would it be desirable even if we could do it. I think there might be very limited areas where maybe you would want slower technological progress. You don't, I think, want faster progress in bioweapons, or in, say, isotope separation, that would make it easier to create nukes.

Possibly, there is the first part, the not feasible. If you think it would be desirable to stop it, there's the problem of feasibility.

it would be desirable, for example, maybe to have DNA synthesis machines, not as a product where each lab has their own device, but maybe as a service. Maybe there could be four or five places in the world where you send in your digital blueprint and the DNA comes back, right? And then, you would have the ability, if one day it really looked like it was necessary, we would have like, a finite set of choke points. So I think you want to look for kind of special opportunities, where you could have tighter control.

That looks plausible under current conditions. It's not just synthetic biology, either. I mean, any kind of profound, new change in the world could turn out to be a black ball.

I think, has only limited potential. So, with the Type-1 vulnerability again, I mean, if you could reduce the number of people who are incentivized to destroy the world, if only they could get access and the means, that would be good.

I think it's like a hybrid picture. Eliminate can either mean, like, incarcerate or kill, or it can mean persuade them to a better view of the world. But the point is that, suppose you were extremely successful in this, and you reduced the number of such individuals by half. And if you want to do it by persuasion, you are competing against all other powerful forces that are trying to persuade people, parties, religion, education system. But suppose you could reduce it by half, I don't think the risk would be reduced by half. Maybe by five or 10 percent.

I think it's all good to try to deter and persuade people, but we shouldn't rely on that as our only safeguard.

I think there are two general methods that we could use to achieve the ability to stabilize the world against the whole spectrum of possible vulnerabilities. And we probably would need both. So, one is an extremely effective ability to do preventive policing. Such that you could intercept. If anybody started to do this dangerous thing, you could intercept them in real time, and stop them. So this would require ubiquitous surveillance, everybody would be monitored all the time.

You would have maybe AI algorithms, big freedom centers that were reviewing this, etc., etc.

so this little device there, imagine that kind of necklace that you would have to wear at all times with multidirectional cameras. But, to make it go down better, just call it the "freedom tag" or something like that.

there's a whole big conversation on this on its own, obviously. There are huge problems and risks with that, right? We may come back to that. So the other, the final, the other general stabilization capability is kind of plugging another governance gap. So the surveillance would be kind of governance gap at the microlevel, like, preventing anybody from ever doing something highly illegal. Then, there's a corresponding governance gap at the macro level, at the global level. You would need the ability, reliably, to prevent the worst kinds of global coordination failures, to avoid wars between great powers, arms races, cataclysmic commons problems, in order to deal with the Type-2a vulnerabilities.

It's certainly true that the scale of political organization has increased over the course of human history. It used to be hunter-gatherer band, right, and then chiefdom, city-states, nations, now there are international organizations and so on and so forth. Again, I just want to make sure I get the chance to stress that obviously there are huge downsides and indeed, massive risks, both to mass surveillance and to global governance. I'm just pointing out that if we are lucky, the world could be such that these would be the only ways you could survive a black ball.

I think it is an option, a very tempting option, it's in a sense the easiest option and it might work, but it means we are fundamentally vulnerable to extracting a black ball. Now, I think with a bit of coordination, like, if you did solve this macrogovernance problem, and the microgovernance problem, then we could extract all the balls from the urn and we'd benefit greatly.

On an individual level, we seem to kind of be doomed anyway, just with the time line, we're rotting and aging and all kinds of things, right?

It's actually a little bit tricky. If you want to set up so that you can attach a probability, first, who are we? If you're very old, probably you'll die of natural causes, if you're very young, you might have a 100-year -- the probability might depend on who you ask. Then the threshold, like, what counts as civilizational devastation? In the paper I don't require an existential catastrophe in order for it to count. This is just a definitional matter, I say a billion dead, or a reduction of world GDP by

50 percent, but depending on what you say the threshold is, you get a different probability estimate. But I guess you could put me down as a frightened optimist.

Chapter 5

Nationalism and Globalism [1]

Nationalism or globalism -- what is the best path forward? This question impacts everything we care about: our cultural identity, our prosperity, our political systems -- everything -- the health of our planet -- everything.

So, on the one hand, we have nationalism. Collins defines it as a "devotion to one's nation," but also, a "doctrine that puts national interests above international considerations." For nationalists, our modern societies are built on national grounds: we share a land, a history, a culture, and we defend each other. In a big and chaotic world, they see nationalism as the only sensible way to maintain social stability. But alarmed globalists warn us: self-centered nationalism can easily turn ugly. We've seen it with 20th-century fascisms: bloody wars, millions of deaths, immeasurable destruction.

On the other hand, we have globalism. The Oxford Living Dictionary defines it as: "the operation or planning of economic and foreign policy on a global basis." For nationalists, globalism is rapidly deconstructing what our ancestors took decades to build. It's like spitting on our soldiers'

)[1] Wanis Kabbaj: TED@UPS

tombs; it's eroding our national solidarities and opening the doors to foreign invasions. But globalists make the case that reinforcing our global governance is the only way to tackle big super national problems, like nuclear proliferation, the global refugee crisis, climate change or terrorism or even the consequences of superhuman AI. So, we are at the crossroads, and we are asked to choose: nationalism or globalism?

Having lived in four continents, I've always been interested in this question. But it took a whole new level when I saw this happening: the biggest surge in nationalist votes in Western democracies since World War II. All of a sudden, this isn't theory anymore. I mean, these political movements have built their success with ideas that could mean, down the road, losing my French citizenship because I'm North African or not being able to come back home to the US because I come from a Muslim-majority country.

when you live in a democracy, you live with this idea that your government will always protect you, as long as you abide by the laws. With the rise of national populism, despite being the best citizen I can, I now have to live with the idea that my government can hurt me for reasons I cannot control. It's very unsettling. But it forced me to rethink and rethink this question and try to think deeper. And the more I thought about it, the more I started questioning the question. Why would we have to choose between nationalism and globalism, between loving our country and caring for the world? There's no reason for that. We don't have to choose between family and country or region or religion and country. We already have multiple identities, and we live with them very well. Why would we have to choose between country and world? What if, instead of accepting this absurd choice, we took it on ourselves to fight this dangerous, binary thinking?

So, for all the globalists in the audience, I want to ask: When I say the word "nationalist," what image comes to your mind? Something like this? Believe me, I think of that, too. But I'd like you to remember that for most people, nationalism feels more like this. Or maybe like that. You know, it's that thing inside you when you accidentally watch an obscure Olympic sport on TV -- and the mere sight of an unknown athlete wearing your national colors gets you all excited. Your heartbeat goes up, your stress level goes up, and you're standing in front of the TV and screaming with passion for that athlete to win. That's nationalism. It's people happy to be together, happy to belong to a large national community. Why would it be wrong?

You know, globalists, you may think of nationalism as an old, 19th-century idea that is destined to fade. But I'm sorry to tell you that the facts are not on your side. When the World Values Survey asked more than 89,000 people across 60 countries how proud they felt about their country, 88.5 percent said "very proud" or "quite proud" -- 88.5 percent. Nationalism is not going away anytime soon. It's a powerful feeling that, according to another study, is a strong predictor of individual happiness. It's crazy, but your happiness is more correlated with national satisfaction than with things you would expect, like household income or your job satisfaction or your health satisfaction. So, if nationalism makes people happy, why would anybody take it away from them?

Fellow globalists, if you are like me, you may be attached to globalization for humanistic reasons. And you may take great joy in some of its accomplishments since 1945. After all, major regions of the world have been exceptionally peaceful; extreme poverty rates around the globe are trending down; and more than two billion people, most notably in Asia, show spectacular improvements in their standards of living. But studies also show that globalization has a dark side. And left on the side of the road are hundreds of millions of people in Western middle classes with anemic income growth for more than two decades, possibly three decades, according to some studies. We cannot ignore this elephant in our room. If anything, our collective energy would be better used finding ways to fix this aspect of globalization, instead of fighting this polarizing battle against nationalism.

71 percent of the world population agreed with the statement, "I am a citizen of the world." Do you know what it means? Most of us are simultaneously proud of our country and citizens of the world. And it gets even better. The citizens of the world in the survey show a higher level of national pride than the ones that rejected that label. So once and for all, being a globalist doesn't mean betraying your country. It just means that you have enough social empathy, and you project some of it outside your national borders.

I know that when I dig into my own nationalist feelings, one of my anxieties versus the globalized world is national identity: How are we going to preserve what makes us special, what makes us different, what brings us together? And as I started thinking about it, I realized something really strange, which is that a lot of the key ingredients of our national identities actually come from outside our national borders. Like, think of the letters that we use every day.

And there are so many other examples. Take the United Kingdom and its monarchy. Queen Elizabeth II? German ancestry. The mottos on the royal coat of arms? All written in French, not a single word of English. Take France and it's iconic Eiffel Tower.

This was the tallest building in New York in the mid-19th century. Does it remind you of something? And you may think of China as a self-contained civilization, protected behind its Great Wall. But think twice. The Chinese official ideology? Marxism, made in Germany. One of China's biggest religions? Buddhism, imported from India. India's favorite pastime? Cricket. I really love this quote from Ashis Nandy, who said, "Cricket is an Indian game accidentally discovered by the British."

So these are good reminders that a lot of what we love in our national traditions actually come from previous waves of globalization. And beyond individual symbols, there are whole national traditions that could not have existed without globalization. And the example that comes to my mind is a world-beloved national tradition: Italian cuisine. My friends, if you ever have a chance to go to a super authentic Italian restaurant that only serves ancient Roman recipes, my advice for you is: don't go.

You'd get very, very disappointed. No spaghetti, no pasta -- that really started in Sicily in the eighth century, when it was under Arabian rule. No perfect espresso, no creamy cappuccino -- that came from Abyssinia via Yemen in the 17th century. And of course, no perfect pizza Napoletana -- how would you make it without the tomatoes of the New World? No, instead, you would be served probably a lot of porridge, some vegetable -- mostly cabbage -- some cheese, and maybe if you're lucky, the absolute delicacy of that time - - mmm, perfectly cooked fattened dormice.

Thankfully, it was not a close tradition preserved by fanatic watchdogs. No, it was an open process, nourished by explorers, traders, street sellers and innovative home cooks. And in many ways, globalization is a chance for our national traditions to be questioned, regenerated, reinterpreted, to attract new converts to stay vibrant and relevant over time.

So just remember this: most of us nationalists in the world are globalists, and most of us globalists in the world are nationalists. A lot of what we like in our national traditions come from outside our national borders. And the reason we venture outside our national borders is to discover these other national traditions. So, the real question should not be to choose between nationalism and globalism. The real question is: How can we do both better? It's a complex question for a complex world that calls for creative, nonbinary solutions.

Chapter 6

Global ethic vs. national interest [1]

It is about global citizenship and recognizing our responsibilities to others. There is so much to do over the next few years that is obvious to so many of us to build a better world. And there is so much shared sense of what we need to do, that it is vital that we all come together. But we don't necessarily have the means to do so.

So, there are challenges to be met. I believe the concept of global citizenship will simply grow out of people talking to each other across continents. But of course, the task is to create the institutions that make that global society work. But I don't think we should underestimate the extent to which massive changes in technology make possible the linking up of people across the world.

of course, national identity remains important. But it's not at the expense of people accepting their global responsibilities. And I think one of the problems of recession is that people become more protectionist, they look in on themselves, they try to protect their own nation, perhaps at the expense of other nations. When you actually look at the motor of the world economy, it cannot move forward unless there is trade between the

---

)[1] Gordon Brown: Britain's former prime minister

different countries. And any nation that would become protectionist over the next few years would deprive itself of the chance of getting the benefits of growth in the world economy.

So, you've got to have a healthy sense of patriotism; that's absolutely important. But you've got to realize that this world has changed fundamentally, and the problems we have cannot be solved by one nation and one nation alone.

I think we can persuade people that what is necessary for Britain's long-term interests, what is necessary for America's long-term interests, is proper engagement with the rest of the world, and taking the action that is necessary.

There is a great story, again, told about Richard Nixon. 1958, Ghana becomes independent, so it is just over 50 years ago. Richard Nixon goes to represent the United States government at the celebrations for independence in Ghana. And it's one of his first outings as Vice President to an African country. He doesn't quite know what to do, so he starts going around the crowd and starts talking to people and he says to people in this rather unique way, "How does it feel to be free?" And he's going around, "How does it feel to be free?" "How does it feel to be free?" And then someone says, "How should I know? I come from Alabama."

And that was the 1950s. Now, what is remarkable is that civil rights in America were achieved in the 1960s. But what is equally remarkable is socioeconomic rights in Africa have not moved forward very fast even since the age of colonialism. And yet, America and Africa have got a common interest. And we have got to realize that if we don't link up with those people who are sensible voices and democratic voices in Africa, to work together for common causes, then the danger of Al Qaeda and related groups making progress in Africa is very big.

So, I would say that what seems sometimes to be altruism, in relation to Africa, or in relation to developing countries, is more than that. It is enlightened self-interest for us to work with other countries. And I would say that national interest and, if you like, what is the global interest to tackle poverty and climate change do, in the long run, come together. And whatever the short-run price for taking action on climate change or on security, or taking action to provide opportunities for people for education, these are prices that are worth paying so that you build a stronger global society where people feel able to feel comfortable with each other and are able to communicate with each other in such a way that you can actually build stronger links between different countries.

I do agree that my responsibility is first of all to make sure that people in our country are safe. And I wouldn't like anything that is said today to suggest that I am diminishing the importance of the responsibility that each leader has for their own country.

But I'm trying to suggest that there is a huge opportunity open to us that was never open to us before. But the power to communicate across borders allows us to organize the world in a different way. And I think, look at the tsunami, it's a classic example. Where was the early warning systems? Where was the world acting together to deal with the problems that they knew arose from the potential for earthquakes, as well as the potential for climate change? And when the world starts to work together, with better early-warning systems, you can deal with some of these problems in a better way. I just think we're not seeing, at the moment, the huge opportunities open to us by the ability of people to cooperate in a world where either there was isolationism before or there was limited alliances based on convenience which never actually took you to deal with some of the central problems.

I think every religion, every faith, and I'm not just talking here to people of faith or religion -- it has this global ethic at the center of its credo. And whether it's Jewish or whether it's Muslim or whether it's Hindu, or whether it's Sikh, the same global ethic is at the heart of each of these religions. So, I think you're dealing with something that people instinctively see as part of their moral sense. So you're building on something that is not pure self-interest. You're building on people's ideas and values -- that perhaps they're candles that burn very dimly on certain occasions. But it is a set of values that cannot, in my view, be extinguished.

Then the question is, how do you make that change happen? How do you persuade people that it is in their interest to build strong -- After the Second World War, we built institutions, the United Nations, the IMF, the World Bank, the World Trade Organization, the Marshall Plan? There was a period in which people talked about an act of creation, because these institutions were so new. But they are now out of date. They don't deal with the problems. You can't deal with the environmental problem through existing institutions. You can't deal with the security problem in the way that you need to. You can't deal with the economic and financial problem. So, we have got to rebuild our global institutions, build them in a way that is suitable to the challenges of this time.

And I believe that if you look at the biggest challenge we face, it is to persuade people to have the confidence that we can build a truly global society with the institutions that are founded on these rules. So, I come back to my initial point. Sometimes you think things are impossible. Nobody would have said 50 years ago that apartheid would have gone in 1990, or that the Berlin wall would have fallen at the turn of the '80s and '90s, or that polio could be eradicated, or perhaps 60 years ago, nobody would have said a man could gone to the Moon. All these things have happened. By tackling the impossible, you make the impossible possible.

We have a responsibility to protect. I mean look, 1918, the Treaty of Versailles, and all the treaties before that, the Treaty of Westphalia and everything else, were about protecting the sovereign right of countries to do what they want. Since then, the world has moved forward, partly as a result of what happened with the Holocaust, and people's concern about the rights of individuals within territories where they need protection, partly because of what we saw in Rwanda, partly because of what we saw in Bosnia. The idea of the responsibility to protect all individuals who are in situations where they are at humanitarian risk is now being established as a principle which governs the world.

So, while I can't automatically say that Britain will rush to the aid of any citizen of any country, in danger, I can say that Britain is in a position where we're working with other countries so that this idea that you have a responsibility to protect people who are victims of either genocide or humanitarian attack, is something that is accepted by the whole world.

Now, in the end, that can only be achieved if your international institutions work well enough to be able to do so. And that comes back to what the future role of the United Nations, and what it can do, actually is. But, the responsibility to protect is a new idea that is, in a sense, taken over from the idea of self-determination as the principle governing the international community.

We're saying that you cannot solve the problem of climate change in one country; you've got to involve all countries. You're saying that you must, and you have a duty to help those countries that cannot afford to deal with the problems of climate change themselves. You're saying you want a deal with all the different countries of the world where we're all bound together to cutting carbon emissions in a way that is to the benefit of the whole world. We've never had this before because Kyoto didn't work. If you could get a deal at Copenhagen, where people agreed, A, that there was a long-term target for carbon emission cuts, B, that there was short-range targets that had to be met so this wasn't just abstract; it was people actually making decisions now that would make a difference now, and if you could then find a financing mechanism that meant that the poorest countries that had been hurt by our inability to deal with climate change over many, many years and decades are given special help so that they can move to energy-efficient technologies, and they are in a position financially to be able to afford the long-term investment that is associated with cutting carbon emissions, then you are treating the world equally, by giving consideration to every part of the planet and the needs they have.

It doesn't mean that everybody does exactly the same thing, because we've actually got to do more financially to help the poorest countries, but it does mean there is equal consideration for the needs of citizens in a single planet.

I think Europe has got a position, which is 27 countries have already come together. I mean, the great difficulty in Europe is if you're at a meeting and 27 people speak, it takes a very, very long time. But we did get an agreement on climate change. America has made its first disposition on this with the bill that President Obama should be congratulated for getting through Congress. Japan has made an announcement. China and India have signed up to the scientific evidence. And now we've got to move them to accept a long-term target, and then short-term targets. But more progress has been made, I think, in the last few weeks than had been made for some years.

And I do believe that there is a strong possibility that if we work together, we can get that agreement to Copenhagen. I certainly have been putting forward proposals that would have allowed the poorest parts of the world to feel that we have taken into account their specific needs. And we would help them adapt. And we would help them make the transition to a low-carbon economy.

I do think a reform of the international institutions is vital to this. When the IMF was created in the 1940s, it was created with resources that were five percent or so of the world's GDP. The IMF now has limited resources, one percent. It can't really make the difference that ought to be made in a period of crisis. So, we've got to rebuild the world institutions. And that's a big task: persuading all the different countries with the different voting shares in these institutions to do so.

It is very important to recognize that this reform of institutions is the next stage after agreeing upon ourselves that there is a clear ethic upon which we can build.

Chapter 7

Global response after 9/11 [1]

Almost 20 years have passed since 9/11. It is time to take stock of where we stand and stop and think. It is time to ask ourselves, have the assumptions and policies we developed in the wake of those tragic events truly made us more secure? Have they made our societies, both in Europe and in the United States, more resilient?

I've worked all my life in the field of security and defense, and I am convinced that now, more than ever, we need to radically reframe the way we think and act about security, and especially about international security. By international security, I actually mean what we do, how we prepare our countries to better respond and prevent external threats, and how we protect our citizens. The key to both is to focus on protecting civilians, both in our own countries and in those where we are present in the name of security.

Now, this idea goes against the fixed narrative that we developed over the past 20 years over what security is and how to get it, but that narrative is flawed, and worse, it is counterproductive. Over the past 20 years, both in the United States and in Europe, we've come to accept that we must talk about security in

---

)[1] benedetta berti: conflict and security researcher.

zero sum terms, as if the only way to gain more security is by compromising on values and rights: security versus human rights, safety versus freedom and development. This is a false opposition. It just doesn't work like that. We need to recognize that security and human rights are not opposite values, they are intrinsically related. After all, the most basic human right is the right to live and to be free from violence, and a state's most basic responsibility is to guarantee that right for its citizens. Conversely, if we think about communities all over the world affected by war and conflict, it is insecurity and violence that stops them from achieving their full freedom and development. Now, they need basic security just as much as we do and they need it so they can live a normal life and so that they can enjoy their human rights.

This is why we need to shift. We need to acknowledge that sustainable security builds on a foundation of human rights, builds on promoting and respecting human rights.

Also, over the past two decades, we have accepted that the best way to guarantee our own security is by defeating our enemies, and to do that, we need to rely almost exclusively on the military. Again, this clashes with my work, with my research, with what I see in the field. What I see is that building sustainable security has a lot less to do with crushing enemies, has a lot less to do with winning on the battlefield, and has a lot more to do with protecting victims and building stability. And to do that, well, the military alone is simply insufficient.

This is why I believe we need to shelve the never-ending War on Terror, and we need to replace it with a security agenda that is driven by the principle of protecting civilians, no matter where they are from, what passport they hold, or where they live: Vancouver, New York, Kabul, Mosul, Aleppo or Douma. Sustainable security tells us that we're more likely to have long-term security at home for ourselves if we focus our engagements abroad on protecting civilians and on ensuring their lives are lived in dignity and free from violence.

For example, we all know that defeating ISIS is a security achievement. Absolutely. But rebuilding destroyed homes, restoring order, ensuring a representative political system, these are just as, if not more important, and not just for the security of civilians in Iraq and in Syria, but for our own security and for global stability.

More fundamentally, ISIS's danger should not just be counted in the number of weapons it holds but also in the number of children it has kept out of school or indoctrinated. This is from a security perspective. From a security perspective, the long-term generational impact of having millions of children in Syria growing up knowing only war and out of school, this is a far more dangerous threat to stability than all of ISIS's weapons combined, and we should spend just as much time and just as much energy to counter this as what we spend when countering ISIS militarily.

Over the past two decades, our security policy has been short-term. It has focused on the here and now. It has systematically downplayed the link between what we do today in the name of security and the long-term impact of those choices. In the years after 9/11, some of the choices, some of the policies we've implemented have probably made us less, not more secure in the long term. Sustainable, civilian-centered security needs to look at what happens in the long term. Again, for example, relying on drones to target enemies in faraway countries may be a tool. It may be a tool to make sure or to lessen the threat of an imminent attack on the United States. But what about the long-term impact? If civilians are killed, if communities are targeted, this will feed a vicious circle of war, conflict, trauma and radicalization, and that vicious circle is at the center of so many of the security challenges we face today. This will not make us safer in the long term.

We need civilian security, we need sustainable civilian-centered security, and we need it now. We need to encourage thinking and research around this concept, and to implement it.

We live in a dangerous world. We have many threats to peace and conflict. Much like in the days after 9/11, we simply cannot afford not to think about international security. But we have to learn the lessons of the past 20 years. To get it right, to get security right, we need to focus on the long term. We need to focus on protecting civilians. And we need to respect and acknowledge the fact that sustainable security builds on a foundation of human rights. Otherwise, in the name of security, we risk leaving the world a far more dangerous and unstable place than what we already found it in.

Chapter 8

The global power shift [1]

There's a poem written by a very famous English poet at the end of the 19th century. It was said to echo in Churchill's brain in the 1930s. And the poem goes: "On the idle hill of summer, lazy with the flow of streams, hark I hear a distant drummer, drumming like a sound in dreams, far and near and low and louder on the roads of earth go by, dear to friend and food to powder, soldiers marching, soon to die." Those who are interested in poetry, the poem is "A Shropshire Lad" written by A.E. Housman.

But what Housman understood, and you hear it in the symphonies of Nielsen too, was that the long, hot, silvan summers of stability of the 19th century were coming to a close, and that we were about to move into one of those terrifying periods of history when power changes. And these are always periods, ladies and gentlemen, accompanied by turbulence, and all too often by blood.

And my message for you is that I believe we are condemned, if you like, to live at just one of those moments in history when the gimbals upon which the established order of power is

---

)[1] paddy ashdown: a former member of the british parliament.

beginning to change and the new look of the world, the new powers that exist in the world, are beginning to take form. And these are -- and we see it very clearly today -- nearly always highly turbulent times, highly difficult times, and all too often very bloody times. By the way, it happens about once every century.

You might argue that the last time it happened -- and that's what Housman felt coming and what Churchill felt too -- was that when power passed from the old nations, the old powers of Europe, across the Atlantic to the new emerging power of the United States of America -- the beginning of the American century. And of course, into the vacuum where the too-old European powers used to be were played the two bloody catastrophes of the last century -- the one in the first part and the one in the second part: the two great World Wars. Mao Zedong used to refer to them as the European civil wars, and it's probably a more accurate way of describing them.

Well, ladies and gentlemen, we live at one of those times. But for us, I want to talk about three factors today. And the first of these, the first two of these, is about a shift in power. And the second is about some new dimension which I want to refer to, which has never quite happened in the way it's happening now. But let's talk about the shifts of power that are occurring to the world. And what is happening today is, in one sense, frightening because it's never happened

before. We have seen lateral shifts of power --
the power of Greece passed to Rome and the
power shifts that occurred during the European
civilizations -- but we are seeing something
slightly different. For power is not just moving
laterally from nation to nation. It's also moving
vertically.

What's happening today is that the
power that was encased, held to accountability,
held to the rule of law, within the institution of
the nation state has now migrated in very large
measure onto the global stage. The globalization
of power -- we talk about the globalization of
markets, but actually it's the globalization of
real power. And where, at the nation state
level that power is held to accountability subject
to the rule of law, on the international stage it is
not. The international stage and the global stage
where power now resides: the power of the
Internet, the power of the satellite
broadcasters, the power of the money changers -
- this vast money-go-round that circulates now
32 times the amount of money necessary for the
trade it's supposed to be there to finance -- the
money changers, if you like, the financial
speculators that have brought us all to our knees
quite recently, the power of the multinational
corporations now developing budgets often
bigger than medium-sized countries. These live
in a global space which is largely
unregulated, not subject to the rule of law, and
in which people may act free of constraint.

Now that suits the powerful up to a moment. It's always suitable for those who have the most power to operate in spaces without constraint, but the lesson of history is that, sooner or later, unregulated space -- space not subject to the rule of law -- becomes populated, not just by the things you wanted -- international trade, the Internet, etc. -- but also by the things you don't want -- international criminality, international terrorism. The revelation of 9/11 is that even if you are the most powerful nation on earth, nevertheless, those who inhabit that space can attack you even in your most iconic of cities one bright September morning. It's said that something like 60 percent of the four million dollars that was taken to fund 9/11 actually passed through the institutions of the Twin Towers which 9/11 destroyed. You see, our enemies also use this space -- the space of mass travel, the Internet, satellite broadcasters -- to be able to get around their poison, which is about destroying our systems and our ways.

Sooner or later, sooner or later, the rule of history is that where power goes governance must follow. And if it is therefore the case, as I believe it is, that one of the phenomenon of our time is the globalization of power, then it follows that one of the challenges of our time is to bring governance to the global space. And I believe that the decades ahead of us now will be to a greater or lesser extent turbulent the more or less we are able to achieve that aim: to bring governance to the global space.

Now notice, I'm not talking about government. I'm not talking about setting up some global democratic institution. My own view, by the way, ladies and gentlemen, is that this is unlikely to be done by spawning more U.N. institutions. If we didn't have the U.N., we'd have to invent it. The world needs an international forum. It needs a means by which you can legitimize international action. But when it comes to governance of the global space, my guess is this won't happen through the creation of more U.N. institutions. It will actually happen by the powerful coming together and making treaty-based systems, treaty-based agreements, to govern that global space.

And if you look, you can see them happening, already beginning to emerge. The World Trade Organization: treaty-based organization, entirely treaty-based, and yet, powerful enough to hold even the most powerful, the United States, to account if necessary. Kyoto: the beginnings of struggling to create a treaty-based organization. The G20: we know now that we have to put together an institution which is capable of bringing governance to that financial space for financial speculation. And that's what the G20 is, a treaty-based institution.

Now there's a problem there, and we'll come back to it in a minute, which is that if you bring the most powerful together to make the rules in treaty-based institutions, to fill that governance space, then what happens to the weak who are left out? And that's a big problem, and we'll return to it in just a second.

So, there's my first message, that if you are to pass through these turbulent times more or less turbulently, then our success in doing that will in large measure depend on our capacity to bring sensible governance to the global space. And watch that beginning to happen. My second point is, and I know I don't have to talk to an audience like this about such a thing, but power is not just shifting vertically, it's also shifting horizontally.

You might argue that the story, the history of civilizations, has been civilizations gathered around seas -- with the first ones around the Mediterranean, the more recent ones in the ascendants of Western power around the Atlantic. Well it seems to me that we're now seeing a fundamental shift of power, broadly speaking, away from nations gathered around the Atlantic [seaboard] to the nations gathered around the Pacific rim. Now that begins with economic power, but that's the way it always begins. You already begin to see the development of foreign policies, the augmentation of military budgets occurring in the other growing powers in the world. I think actually this is not so much a shift from the West to the East; something different is happening.

My guess is, for what it's worth, is that the United States will remain the most powerful nation on earth for the next 10 years, 15, but the context in which she holds her power has now radically altered; it has radically changed. We are coming out of 50 years, most unusual years, of history in which we have had a totally mono-polar world, in which every compass needle for or against has to be referenced by its position to Washington -- a world bestrode by a single colossus. But that's not a usual case in history. In fact, what's now emerging is the much more normal case of history. You're beginning to see the emergence of a multi-polar world.

Up until now, the United States has been the dominant feature of our world. They will remain the most powerful nation, but they will be the most powerful nation in an increasingly multi-polar world. And you begin to see the alternative centers of power building up -- in China, of course, though my own guess is that China's ascent to greatness is not smooth. It's going to be quite grumpy as China begins to democratize her society after liberalizing her economy. But that's a subject of a different discussion. You see India, you see Brazil. You see increasingly that the world now looks actually, for us Europeans, much more like Europe in the 19th century.

Europe in the 19th century: a great British foreign secretary, Lord Canning, used to describe it as the "European concert of powers." There was a balance, a five-sided balance. Britain always played to the balance. If Paris got together with Berlin, Britain got together with Vienna and Rome to provide a counterbalance. Now notice, in a period which is dominated by a mono-polar world, you have fixed alliances -- NATO, the Warsaw Pact. A fixed polarity of power means fixed alliances. But a multiple polarity of power means shifting and changing alliances. And that's the world we're coming into, in which we will increasingly see that our alliances are not fixed. Canning, the great British foreign secretary once said, "Britain has a common interest, but no common allies." And we will see increasingly that even we in the West will reach out, have to reach out, beyond the cozy circle of the Atlantic powers to make alliances with others if we want to get things done in the world.

Note, that when we went into Libya, it was not good enough for the West to do it alone; we had to bring others in. We had to bring, in this case, the Arab League in. My guess is Iraq and Afghanistan are the last times when the West has tried to do it themselves, and we haven't succeeded. My guess is that we're reaching the beginning of the end of 400 years -- I say 400 years because it's the end of the Ottoman Empire -- of the hegemony of Western power, Western institutions and Western values. You know, up until now, if the West got its act together, it could propose and dispose in every corner of the world. But that's no longer true. Take the last financial crisis after the Second World War. The West got together -- the Bretton Woods Institution, World Bank, International Monetary Fund -- the problem solved. Now we have to call in others. Now we have to create the G20. Now we have to reach beyond the cozy circle of our Western friends.

Let me make a prediction for you, which is probably even more startling. I suspect we are now reaching the end of 400 years when Western power was enough. People say to me, "The Chinese, of course, they'll never get themselves involved in peace-making, multilateral peace-making around the world." Oh yes? Why not? How many Chinese troops are serving under the blue beret, serving under the blue flag, serving under the U.N. command in the world today? 3,700. How many Americans? 11. What is the largest naval contingent tackling the issue of Somali pirates? The Chinese naval contingent. Of course, they are, they are a mercantilist nation. They want to keep the sea lanes open. Increasingly, we are going to have to do business with people with whom we do not share values, but with whom, for the moment, we share common interests. It's a whole new different way of looking at the world that is now emerging.

And here's the third factor, which is totally different. Today in our modern world, because of the Internet, because of the kinds of things people have been talking about here, everything is connected to everything. We are now interdependent. We are now interlocked, as nations, as individuals, in a way which has never been the case before, never been the case before. The interrelationship of nations, well it's always existed. Diplomacy is about managing the interrelationship of nations. But now we are intimately locked together. You get swine flu in Mexico, it's a problem for Charles de Gaulle Airport 24 hours later. Lehman Brothers goes down, the whole lot collapses. There are fires in the steppes of Russia, food riots in Africa.

We are all now deeply, deeply, deeply interconnected. And what that means is the idea of a nation state acting alone, not connected with others, not working with others, is no longer a viable proposition. Because the actions of a nation state are neither confined to itself, nor is it sufficient for the nation state itself to control its own territory, because the effects outside the nation state are now beginning to affect what happens inside them.

I was a young soldier in the last of the small empire wars of Britain. At that time, the defense of my country was about one thing and one thing only: how strong was our army, how strong was our air force, how strong was our navy and how strong were our allies. That was when the enemy was outside the walls. Now the enemy is inside the walls. Now if I want to talk about the defense of my country, I have to speak to the Minister of Health because pandemic disease is a threat to my security, I have to speak to the Minister of Agriculture because food security is a threat to my security, I have to speak to the Minister of Industry because the fragility of our hi-tech infrastructure is now a point of attack for our enemies -- as we see from cyber warfare -- I have to speak to the Minister of Home Affairs because who has entered my country, who lives in that terraced house in that inner city has a direct effect on what happens in my country -- as we in London saw in the 7/7 bombings. It's no longer the case that the security of a country is simply a matter for its soldiers and its ministry of defense. It's its capacity to lock together its institutions.

And this tells you something very important. It tells you that, in fact, our governments, vertically constructed, constructed on the economic model of the Industrial Revolution -- vertical hierarchy, specialization of tasks, command structures -- have got the wrong structures completely. You in business know that the paradigm structure of our time, ladies and gentlemen, is the network. It's your capacity to network that matters, both within your governments and externally.

So, here is Ashdown's third law. By the way, don't ask me about Ashdown's first law and second law because I haven't invented those yet; it always sounds better if there's a third law, doesn't it? Ashdown's third law is that in the modern age, where everything is connected to everything, the most important thing about what you can do is what you can do with others. The most important bit about your structure -- whether you're a government, whether you're an army regiment, whether you're a business -- is your docking points, your interconnectors, your capacity to network with others. You understand that in industry; governments don't.

But now one final thing. If it is the case, ladies and gentlemen -- and it is -- that we are now locked together in a way that has never been quite the same before, then it's also the case that we share a destiny with each other. Suddenly and for the very first time, collective defense, the thing that has dominated us as the concept of securing our nations, is no longer enough. It used to be the case that if my tribe was more powerful than their tribe, I was safe; if my country was more powerful than their country, I was safe; my alliance, like NATO, was more powerful than their alliance, I was safe. It is no longer the case. The advent of the interconnectedness and of the weapons of mass destruction means that, increasingly, I share a destiny with my enemy.

When I was a diplomat negotiating the disarmament treaties with the Soviet Union in Geneva in the 1970s, we succeeded because we understood we shared a destiny with them. Collective security is not enough. Peace has come to Northern Ireland because both sides realized that the zero-sum game couldn't work. They shared a destiny with their enemies. One of the great barriers to peace in the Middle East is that both sides, both Israel and, I think, the Palestinians, do not understand that they share a collective destiny. And so suddenly, ladies and gentlemen, what has been the proposition of visionaries and poets down the ages becomes something we have to take seriously as a matter of public policy.

I started with a poem; I'll end with one. The great poem of John Donne's. "Send not for whom the bell tolls." The poem is called "No Man is an Island." And it goes: "Every man's death affected me, for I am involved in mankind, send not to ask for whom the bell tolls, it tolls for thee." For John Donne, a recommendation of morality. For us, I think, part of the equation for our survival.

Chapter 9

Understanding power [1]

Why is it that the very word "civics" has such a soporific, even a narcoleptic effect on us? I think it's because the very word signifies something exceedingly virtuous, exceedingly important, and exceedingly boring. Well, I think it's the responsibility of people like us, people who show up for gatherings like this in person or online, in any way we can, to make civics sexy again, as sexy as it was during the American Revolution, as sexy as it was during the Civil Rights Movement. And I believe the way we make civics sexy again is to make explicitly about the teaching of power. The way we do that, I believe, is at the level of the city.

This is what I want to talk about today, and I want to start by defining some terms and then I want to describe the scale of the problem I think we face and then suggest the ways that I believe cities can be the seat of the solution. So, let me start with some definitions. By civics, I simply mean the art of being a pro-social, problem-solving contributor in a self-governing community. Civics is the art of citizenship, what Bill Gates Sr. calls simply showing up for life, and it encompasses

---

)[1] Eric Liu: civic evangelist, CEO of citizen university.

three things: a foundation of values, an understanding of the systems that make the world go round, and a set of skills that allow you to pursue goals and to have others join in that pursuit.

And that brings me to my definition of power, which is simply this: the capacity to make others do what you would have them do. It sounds menacing, doesn't it? We don't like to talk about power. We find it scary. We find it somehow evil. We feel uncomfortable naming it. In the culture and mythology of democracy, power resides with the people. Period. End of story. Any further inquiry not necessary and not really that welcome. Power has a negative moral valence. It sounds Machiavellian inherently. It seems inherently evil. But in fact, power is no more inherently good or evil than fire or physics. It just is. And power governs how any form of government operates, whether a democracy or a dictatorship. And the problem we face today, here in America in particular, but all around the world, is that far too many people are profoundly illiterate in power — what it is, who has it, how it operates, how it flows, what part of it is visible, what part of it is not, why some people have it, why that's compounded. And as a result of this illiteracy, those few who do understand how power operates in civic life, those who understand how a bill becomes a law, yes, but also how a friendship becomes a subsidy, or how a bias becomes a policy, or how a slogan becomes a movement, the people who understand those things wield disproportionate influence, and they're perfectly happy to fill the vacuum created by the ignorance of the great majority.

This is why it is so fundamental for us right now to grab hold of this idea of power and to democratize it. One of the things that is so profoundly exciting and challenging about this moment is that as a result of this power illiteracy that is so pervasive, there is a concentration of knowledge, of understanding, of clout. I mean, think about it: How does a friendship become a subsidy? Seamlessly, when a senior government official decides to leave government and become a lobbyist for a private interest and convert his or her relationships into capital for their new masters. How does a bias become a policy? Insidiously, just the way that stop-and-frisk, for instance, became over time a bureaucratic numbers game. How does a slogan become a movement? Virally, in the way that the Tea Party, for instance, was able to take the "Don't Tread on Me" flag from the American Revolution, or how, on the other side, a band of activists could take a magazine headline, "Occupy Wall Street," and turn that into a global meme and movement. The thing is, though, most people aren't looking for and don't want to see these realities. So much of this ignorance, this civic illiteracy, is willful. There are some millennials, for instance, who think the whole business is just sordid. They don't want to have anything to do with politics. They'd rather just opt out and engage in volunteerism. There are some techies out there who believe that the cure-all for any power imbalance or power abuse is simply more data, more transparency. There are some on the left who think power resides only with corporations, and some on the right who think power resides only with government, each side blinded by their selective outrage. There are the naive who believe that good things just happen and the cynical who believe that bad things just happen, the fortunate and unfortunate alike who think that their lot is simply what they deserve rather than the eminently alterable result of a prior arrangement, an inherited allocation, of power.

As a result of all of this creeping fatalism in public life, we here, particularly in America today, have depressingly low levels of civic knowledge, civic engagement, participation, awareness. The whole business of politics has been effectively subcontracted out to a band of professionals, money people, outreach people, message people, research people. The rest of us are meant to feel like amateurs in the sense of suckers. We become demotivated to learn more about how things work. We begin to opt out.

Well, this problem, this challenge, is a thing that we must now confront, and I believe that when you have this kind of disengagement, this willful ignorance, it becomes both a cause and a consequence of this concentration of opportunity of wealth and clout that I was describing a moment ago, this profound civic inequality. This is why it is so important in our time right now to reimagine civics as the teaching of power. Perhaps it's never been more important at any time in our lifetimes. If people don't learn power, people don't wake up, and if they don't wake up, they get left out.

Now, part of the art of practicing power means being awake and having a voice, but it also is about having an arena where you can plausibly practice deciding. All of civics boils down to the simple question of who decides, and you have to play that out in a place, in an arena.

And this brings me to the third point that I want to make today, which is simply that there is no better arena in our time for the practicing of power than the city. Think about the city where you live, where you're from. Think about a problem in the common life of your city. It can be something small, like where a street lamp should go, or something medium like which library should have its hours extended or cut, or maybe something bigger, like whether a dilapidated waterfront should be turned into a highway or a greenway, or whether all the businesses in your town should be required to pay a living wage. Think about the change that you want in your city, and then think about how you would get it, how you would make it happen. Take an inventory of all the forms of power that are at play in your city's situation: money, of course, people, yes, ideas, information, misinformation, the threat of force, the force of norms. All of these forms of power are at play. Now think about how you would activate or perhaps neutralize these various forms of power.

This is not some Game of Thrones empire-level set of questions. These are questions that play out in every single place on the planet. I'll just tell you quickly about two stories drawn from recent headlines. In Boulder, Colorado, voters not too long ago approved a process to replace the private power company, literally the power company, the electric company Xcel, with a publicly owned utility that would forego profits and attend far more to climate change. Well, Xcel fought back, and Xcel has now put in play a ballot measure that would undermine or undo this municipalization. And so, the citizen activists in Boulder who have been pushing this now literally have to fight the power in order to fight for power. In Tuscaloosa, at the University of Alabama, there's an organization on campus called, kind of menacingly, the Machine, and it draws from largely white sororities and fraternities on campus, and for decades, the Machine has dominated student government elections. Well now, recently, the Machine has started to get involved in actual city politics, and they've engineered the election of a former Machine member, a young, pro-business recent graduate to the Tuscaloosa city school board. Now, as I say, these are just two examples drawn almost at random from the headlines. Every day, there are thousands more like them. And you may like or dislike the efforts I'm describing here in Boulder or in Tuscaloosa, but you cannot help but admire the power literacy of the players involved, their skill. You cannot help but reckon with and recognize the command they have of the elemental questions of civic power — what objective, what strategy, what tactics, what is the terrain, who are your enemies, who are your allies?

Now I want you to return to thinking about that problem or that opportunity or that challenge in your city, and the thing it was that you want to fix or create in your city, and ask yourself, do you have command of these elemental questions of power? Could you put into practice effectively what it is that you know? This is the challenge and the opportunity for us.

We live in a time right now where in spite of globalization or perhaps because of globalization, all citizenship is ever more resonantly, powerfully local. Indeed, power in our time is flowing ever faster to the city. Here in the United States, the national government has tied itself up in partisan knots. Civic imagination and innovation and creativity are emerging from local ecosystems now and radiating outward, and this great innovation, this great wave of localism that's now arriving, and you see it in how people eat and work and share and buy and move and live their everyday lives, this isn't some precious parochialism, this isn't some retreat into insularity, no. This is emergent. The localism of our time is networked powerfully. And so, for instance, consider the ways that strategies for making cities more bike-friendly have spread so rapidly from Copenhagen to New York to Austin to Boston to Seattle. Think about how experiments in participatory budgeting, where everyday citizens get a chance to allocate and decide upon the allocation of city funds. Those experiments have spread from Porto Alegre, Brazil to here in New York City, to the wards of Chicago. Migrant workers from Rome to Los Angeles and many cities between are now organizing to stage strikes to remind the people who live in their cities what a day without immigrants would look like. In China, all across that country, members of the New Citizens' Movement are beginning to activate and organize to fight official corruption and graft, and they're drawing the ire of officials there, but they're also drawing the attention of anti-corruption activists all around the world. In Seattle, where I'm from, we've become part of a great global array of cities that are now working together bypassing government altogether, national government altogether, in order to try to meet the carbon reduction goals of the Kyoto Protocol. All of these citizens, united, are forming a web, a great archipelago of power that allows us to bypass brokenness and monopolies of control.

And our task now is to accelerate this work. Our task now is to bring more and more people into the fold of this work. That's why my organization, Citizen University, has undertaken a project now to create an everyman's curriculum in civic power. And this curriculum starts with this triad that I described earlier of values, systems and skills. And what I'd like to do is to invite all of you to help create this curriculum with the stories and the experiences and the challenges that each of you lives and faces, to create something powerfully collective. And I want to invite you in particular to try a simple exercise drawn from the early frameworks of this curriculum. I want you to write a narrative, a narrative from the future of your city, and you can date it, set it out one year from now, five years from now, a decade from now, a generation from now, and write it as a case study looking back, looking back at the change that you wanted in your city, looking back at the cause that you were championing, and describing the ways that that change and that cause came, in fact, to succeed. Describe the values of your fellow citizens that you activated, and the sense of moral purpose that you were able to stir. Recount all the different ways that you engaged the systems of government, of the marketplace, of social institutions, of faith organizations, of the media. Catalog all the skills you had to deploy, how to negotiate, how to advocate, how to frame issues, how to navigate diversity in conflict, all those skills that enabled you to bring folks on board and to overcome resistance. What you'll be doing when you write that narrative is, you'll be discovering how to read power, and in the process, how to write power. So, share what you write, do you what you write, and then share what you do. I invite you to literally share the narratives that you create on our Facebook page for Citizen University. But even beyond that, it's in the conversations that we have today all around the world in the simultaneous gatherings that are happening on this topic at this moment, and to think about how we can become one another's teachers and students in power. If we do that, then together we can make civics sexy again. Together, we can democratize democracy and make it safe again for amateurs. Together, we can create a great network of city that will be the most powerful collective laboratory for self-government this planet has ever seen. We have the power to do that.

Chapter 10

Pursuing soft power [1]

what worries me is the entire notion of world leadership seems to me terribly archaic. It's redolent of James Bond movies and Kipling ballads. After all, what constitutes a world leader? If it's population, we're on course to top the charts. We will overtake China by 2034. Is it military strength? Well, we have the world's fourth largest army. Is it nuclear capacity? We know we have that. The Americans have even recognized it, in an agreement. Is it the economy? Well, we have now the fifth-largest economy in the world in purchasing power parity terms. And we continue to grow. When the rest of the world took a beating last year, we grew at 6.7 percent.

But, somehow, none of that adds up to me, to what I think India really can aim to contribute in the world, in this part of the 21st century. And so I wondered, could what the future beckons for India to be all about be a combination of these things allied to something else, the power of example, the attraction of India's culture, what, in other words, people like to call "soft power."

Soft power is a concept invented by a Harvard academic, Joseph Nye, a friend of mine. And, very simply, and I'm really cutting it

---

)[1] Shashi Tharoor: India's minister for external affairs.

short because of the time limits here, it's essentially the ability of a country to attract others because of its culture, its political values, its foreign policies. And, you know, lots of countries do this. He was writing initially about the States, but we know the Alliance Francaise is all about French soft power, the British Council. The Beijing Olympics were an exercise in Chinese soft power. Americans have the Voice of America and the Fulbright scholarships. But the fact is, in fact, that probably Hollywood and MTV and McDonalds have done more for American soft power around the world than any specifically government activity.

So soft power is something that really emerges partly because of governments, but partly despite governments. And in the information era we all live in today, what we might call the TED age, I'd say that countries are increasingly being judged by a global public that's been fed on an incessant diet of Internet news, of televised images, of cellphone videos, of email gossip. In other words, all sorts of communication devices are telling us the stories of countries, whether or not the countries concerned want people to hear those stories.

Now, in this age, again, countries with access to multiple channels of communication and information have a particular advantage. And of course, they have more influence, sometimes, about how they're seen. India has more all-news TV channels than any country in the world, in fact in most of the countries in this part of the world put together.

But the fact still is that it's not just that. In order to have soft power, you have to be connected. One might argue that India has become an astonishingly connected country. I think you've already heard the figures. We've been selling 15 million cellphones a month. Currently there are 509 million cellphones in Indian hands, in India. And that makes us larger than the U.S. as a telephone market. In fact, those 15 million cellphones are the most connections that any country, including the U.S. and China, has ever established in the history of telecommunications.

But, what perhaps some of you don't realize is how far we've come to get there. You know, when I grew up in India, telephones were a rarity. In fact, they were so rare that elected members of Parliament had the right to allocate 15 telephone lines as a favor to those they deemed worthy. If you were lucky enough to be a wealthy businessman or an influential journalist, or a doctor or something, you might have a telephone. But sometimes it just sat there.

I went to high school in Calcutta. And we would look at this instrument sitting in the front foyer. But half the time we would pick it up with an expectant look on our faces, there would be no dial tone. If there was a dial tone and you dialed a number, the odds were two in three you wouldn't get the number you were intending to reach. In fact, the words "wrong number" were more popular than the word "Hello." If you then wanted to connect to another city, let's say from Calcutta you wanted to call Delhi, you'd have to book something called a trunk call, and then sit by the phone all day, waiting for it to come through. Or you could pay eight times the going rate for something called a lightning call. But lightning struck rather slowly in our country in those days, so, it was like about a half an hour for a lightning call to come through.

In fact, so woeful was our telephone service that a Member of Parliament stood up in 1984 and complained about this. And the Then-Communications Minister replied in a lordly manner that in a developing country communications are a luxury, not a right, that the government had no obligation to provide better service, and if the honorable Member wasn't satisfied with his telephone, could he please return it, since there was an eight-year-long waiting list for telephones in India.

Now, fast-forward to today and this is what you see: the 15 million cell phones a month. But what is most striking is who is carrying those cell phones. You know, if you visit friends in the suburbs of Delhi, on the side streets you will find a fellow with a cart that looks like it was designed in the 16th century, wielding a coal-fired steam iron that might have been invented in the 18th century. He's called an isthri wala. But he's carrying a 21st-century instrument. He's carrying a cell phone because most incoming calls are free, and that's how he gets orders from the neighborhood, to know where to collect clothes to get them ironed.

The other day I was in Kerala, my home state, at the country farm of a friend, about 20 kilometers away from any place you'd consider urban. And it was a hot day and he said, "Hey, would you like some fresh coconut water?" And it's the best thing and the most nutritious and refreshing thing you can drink on a hot day in the tropics, so I said sure. And he whipped out his cellphone, dialed the number, and a voice said, "I'm up here." And right on top of the nearest coconut tree, with a hatchet in one hand and a cell phone in the other, was a local toddy tapper, who proceeded to bring down the coconuts for us to drink.

Fishermen are going out to sea and carrying their cell phones. When they catch the fish, they call all the market towns along the coast to find out where they get the best possible prices. Farmers now, who used to have to spend half a day of backbreaking labor to find out if the market town was open, if the market was on, whether the product they'd harvested could be sold, what price they'd fetch. They'd often send an eight-year-old boy all the way on this trudge to the market town to get that information and come back, then they'd load the cart. Today they're saving half a day's labor with a two-minute phone call.

So, this empowerment of the underclass is the real result of India being connected. And that transformation is part of where India is heading today. But, of course that's not the only thing about India that's spreading. You've got Bollywood. My attitude to Bollywood is best summarized in the tale of the two goats at a Bollywood garbage dump -- Mr. Shekhar Kapur, forgive me -- and they're chewing away on cans of celluloid discarded by a Bollywood studio. And the first goat, chewing away, says, "You know, this film is not bad." And the second goat says, "No, the book was better."

I usually tend to think that the book is usually better, but, having said that, the fact is that Bollywood is now taking a certain aspect of Indian-ness and Indian culture around the globe, not just in the Indian diaspora in the U.S. and the U.K., but to the screens of Arabs and Africans, of Senegalese and Syrians. I've met a young man in New York whose illiterate mother in a village in Senegal takes a bus once a month to the capital city of Dakar, just to watch a Bollywood movie. She can't understand the dialogue. She's illiterate, so she can't read the French subtitles. But these movies are made to be understood despite such handicaps, and she has a great time in the song and the dance and the action. She goes away with stars in her eyes about India, as a result.

And this is happening more and more. Afghanistan, we know what a serious security problem Afghanistan is for so many of us in the world. India doesn't have a military mission there. You know what was India's biggest asset in Afghanistan in the last seven years? One simple fact: you couldn't try to call an Afghan at 8:30 in the evening. Why? Because that was the moment when the Indian television soap opera, "Kyunki Saas Bhi Kabhi Bahu Thi," dubbed into Dari, was telecast on Tolo T.V. And it was the most popular television show in Afghan history. Every Afghan family wanted to watch it. They had to suspend functions at 8:30. Weddings were reported to be interrupted so guests could cluster around the T.V. set, and then turn their attention back to the bride and groom. Crime went up at 8:30. I have read a Reuters dispatch -- so this is not Indian propaganda, a British news agency -- about how robbers in the town of Musarri Sharif* stripped a vehicle of its windshield wipers, its hubcaps, its sideview mirrors, any moving part they could find, at 8:30, because the watchmen were busy watching the T.V. rather than minding the store. And they scrawled on the windshield in a reference to the show's heroine, "Tulsi Zindabad": "Long live Tulsi."

That's soft power. And that is what India is developing through the "E" part of TED: its own entertainment industry. The same is true, of course -- we don't have time for too many more examples -- but it's true of our music, of our dance, of our art, yoga, ayurveda, even Indian cuisine. I mean, the proliferation of Indian restaurants since I first went abroad as a student, in the mid '70s, and what I see today, you can't go to a mid-size town in Europe or North America and not find an Indian restaurant. It may not be a very good one. But, today in Britain, for example, Indian restaurants in Britain employ more people than the coal mining, ship building and iron and steel industries combined. So the empire can strike back.

But, with this increasing awareness of India, with you and with I, and so on, with tales like Afghanistan, comes something vital in the information era, the sense that in today's world it's not the side of the bigger army that wins, it's the country that tells a better story that prevails. And India is, and must remain, in my view, the land of the better story. Stereotypes are changing. I mean, again, having gone to the U.S. as a student in the mid '70s, I knew what the image of India was then, if there was an image at all.

Today, people in Silicon Valley and elsewhere speak of the IITs, the Indian Institutes of Technology with the same reverence they used to accord to MIT. This can sometimes have unintended consequences. OK. I had a friend, a history major like me, who was accosted at Schiphol Airport in Amsterdam, by an anxiously perspiring

European saying, "You're Indian, you're Indian! Can you help me fix my laptop?"

We've gone from the image of India as land of fakirs lying on beds of nails, and snake charmers with the Indian rope trick, to the image of India as a land of mathematical geniuses, computer wizards, software gurus. But that too is transforming the Indian story around the world. But, there is something more substantive to that. The story rests on a fundamental platform of political pluralism. It's a civilizational story to begin with. Because India has been an open society for millennia. India gave refuge to the Jews, fleeing the destruction of the first temple by the Babylonians, and said thereafter by the Romans.

In fact, legend has is that when Doubting Thomas, the Apostle, Saint Thomas, landed on the shores of Kerala, my home state, somewhere around 52 A.D., he was welcomed on shore by a flute-playing Jewish girl. And to this day remains the only Jewish diaspora in the history of the Jewish people, which has never encountered a single incident of anti-Semitism. That's the Indian story. Islam came peacefully to the south, slightly more differently complicated history in the north. But all of these religions have found a place and a welcome home in India.

we just celebrated, this year, our general elections, the biggest exercise in democratic franchise in human history. And the next one will be even bigger, because our voting population keeps growing by 20 million a year. But, the fact is that the last elections, five years ago, gave the world extraordinary phenomenon of an election being won by a woman political leader of Italian origin and Roman Catholic faith, Sonia Gandhi, who then made way for a Sikh, Mohan Singh, to be sworn in as Prime Minister by a Muslim, President Abdul Kalam, in a country 81 percent Hindu.

This is India, and of course it's all the more striking because it was four years later that we all applauded the U.S., the oldest democracy in the modern world, more than 220 years of free and fair elections, which took till last year to elect a president or a vice president who wasn't white, male or Christian. So, maybe -- oh sorry, he is Christian, I beg your pardon -- and he is male, but he isn't white. All the others have been all those three. (Laughter) All his predecessors have been all those three, and that's the point I was trying to make.

But the issue is that when I talked about that example, it's not just about talking about India, it's not propaganda. Because ultimately, that electoral outcome had nothing to do with the rest of the world. It was essentially India being itself. And ultimately, it seems to me, that always works better than propaganda. Governments aren't very good at telling stories. But people see a society for what it is, and that, it seems to me, is what ultimately will make a difference in today's information era.

So, India now is no longer the nationalism of ethnicity or language or religion, because we have every ethnicity known to mankind, practically, we've every religion known to mankind, with the possible exception of Shintoism, though that has some Hindu elements somewhere. We have 23 official languages that are recognized in our Constitution. And those of you who cashed your money here might be surprised to see how many scripts there are on the rupee note, spelling out the denominations. We've got all of that. We don't even have geography uniting us, because the natural geography of the subcontinent framed by the mountains and the sea was hacked by the partition with Pakistan in 1947. In fact, you can't even take the name of the country for granted, because the name "India" comes from the river Indus, which flows in Pakistan.

But the whole point is that India is the nationalism of an idea. It's the idea of an ever-ever-land, emerging from an ancient civilization, united by a shared history, but sustained, above all, by pluralist democracy. That is a 21st-century story as well as an ancient one. And it's the nationalism of an idea that essentially says you can endure differences of caste, creed, color, culture, cuisine, custom and costume, consonant, for that matter, and still rally around a consensus. And the consensus is of a very simple principle, that in a diverse plural democracy like India you don't really have to agree on everything all the time, so long as you agree on the ground rules of how you will disagree. The great success story of India, a country that so many learned scholars and journalists assumed would disintegrate, in the '50s and '60s, is that it managed to maintain consensus on how to survive without consensus.

Now, that is the India that is emerging into the 21st century. And I do want to make the point that if there is anything worth celebrating about India, it isn't military muscle, economic power. All of that is necessary, but we still have huge amounts of problems to overcome. Somebody said we are super poor, and we are also super power. We can't really be both of those. We have to overcome our poverty. We have to deal with the hardware of development, the ports, the roads, the airports, all the infrastructural things we need to do, and the software of development, the human capital, the need for the ordinary person in India to be able to have a couple of square meals a day, to be able to send his or her children to a decent school, and to aspire to work a job that will give them opportunities in their lives that can transform themselves.

But it's all taking place, this great adventure of conquering those challenges, those real challenges which none of us can pretend

Roshdy Ebrahim

don't exist. But it's all taking place in an open society, in a rich and diverse and plural civilization, in one that is determined to liberate and fulfill the creative energies of its people.

Chapter 11

Can democracy exist without trust? [1]

when you know what to expect, let's give you the story. And this is a rainy election day in a small country -- that can be my country, but could be also your country. And because of the rain until four o'clock in the afternoon, nobody went to the polling stations. But then the rain stopped, people went to vote. And when the votes had been counted, three-fourths of the people have voted with a blank ballot. The government and the opposition, they have been simply paralyzed. Because you know what to do about the protests. You know who to arrest, who to negotiate with. But what to do about people who are voting with a blank ballot? So, the government decided to have the elections once again. And this time even a greater number, 83 percent of the people, voted with blank ballots. Basically, they went to the ballot boxes to tell that they have nobody to vote for.

This is the opening of a beautiful novel by Jose Saramago called "Seeing." But in my view, it very well captures part of the problem that we have with democracy in Europe these days. On one level nobody's questioning that

)[1] ivan Krastev: In Mistrust We Trust: Can Democracy Survive When We Don't Trust Our Leaders? Amazon, 2013

democracy is the best form of government. Democracy is the only game in town. The problem is that many people start to believe that it is not a game worth playing.

For the last 30 years, political scientists have observed that there is a constant decline in electoral turnout, and the people who are least interested to vote are the people whom you expect are going to gain most out of voting. I mean the unemployed, the under-privileged. And this is a major issue. Because especially now with the economic crisis, you can see that the trust in politics, that the trust in democratic institutions, was really destroyed. According to the latest survey being done by the European Commission, 89 percent of the citizens of Europe believe that there is a growing gap between the opinion of the policy-makers and the opinion of the public. Only 18 percent of Italians and 15 percent of Greeks believe that their vote matters. Basically, people start to understand that they can change governments, but they cannot change policies.

And the question which I want to ask is the following: How did it happen that we are living in societies which are much freer than ever before -- we have more rights, we can travel easier, we have access to more information -- at the same time that trust in our democratic institutions basically has collapsed? So basically, I want to ask: What went right and what went wrong in these 50 years when we talk about democracy? And I'll start with what went right.

And the first thing that went right was, of course, these five revolutions which, in my view, very much changed the way we're living and deepened our democratic experience. And the first was the cultural and social revolution of 1968 and 1970s, which put the individual at the center of politics. It was the human rights moment. Basically, this was also a major outbreak, a culture of dissent, a culture of basically non-conformism, which was not known before. So, I do believe that even things like that are very much the children of '68 -- nevertheless that most of us had been even not born then. But after that you have the market revolution of the 1980s. And nevertheless, that many people on the left try to hate it, the truth is that it was very much the market revolution that sent the message: "The government does not know better." And you have more choice-driven societies. And of course, you have 1989 -- the end of Communism, the end of the Cold War. And it was the birth of the global world. And you have the Internet. And this is not the audience to which I'm going to preach to what extent the Internet empowered people. It has changed the way we are communicating and basically, we are viewing politics. The very idea of political community totally has changed. And I'm going to name one more revolution, and this is the revolution in brain sciences, which totally changed the way we understand how people are making decisions.

So, this is what went right. But if we're going to see what went wrong, we're going to end up with the same five revolutions. Because first you have the 1960s and 1970s, cultural and social revolution, which in a certain way destroyed the idea of a collective purpose. The very idea, all these collective nouns that we have been taught about -- nation, class, family. We start to like divorcing, if we're married at all. All this was very much under attack. And it is so difficult to engage people in politics when they believe that what really matters is where they personally stand.

And you have the market revolution of the 1980s and the huge increase of inequality in societies. Remember, until the 1970s, the spread of democracy has always been accompanied by the decline of inequality. The more democratic our societies have been, the more equal they have been becoming. Now we have the reverse tendency. The spread of democracy now is very much accompanied by the increase in inequality. And I find this very much disturbing when we're talking about what's going on right and wrong with democracy these days.

And if you go to 1989 -- something that basically you don't expect that anybody's going to criticize -- but many are going to tell you, "Listen, it was the end of the Cold War that tore the social contract between the elites and the people in Western Europe." When the Soviet Union was still there, the rich and the powerful, they needed the people, because they feared them. Now the elites basically have been liberated. They're very mobile. You cannot tax them. And basically, they don't fear the people. So, as a result of it, you have this very strange situation in which the elites basically got out of the control of the voters. So, this is not by accident that the voters are not interested to vote anymore.

And when we talk about the Internet, yes, it's true, the Internet connected all of us, but we also know that the Internet created these echo chambers and political ghettos in which for all your life you can stay with the political community you belong to. And it's becoming more and more difficult to understand the people who are not like you. I know that many people here have been splendidly speaking about the digital world and the possibility for cooperation, but [have you] seen what the digital world has done to American politics these days? This is also partly a result of the Internet revolution. This is the other side of the things that we like.

And when you go to the brain sciences, what political consultants learned from the brain scientists' is don't talk to me about ideas anymore, don't talk to me about policy programs. What really matters is basically to manipulate the emotions of the people. And you have this very strongly to the extent that, even if you see when we talk about revolutions these days, these revolutions are not named anymore around ideologies or ideas. Before, revolutions used to have ideological names. They could be communist, they could be liberal, they could be fascist or Islamic. Now the revolutions are called under the medium which is most used. You have Facebook revolutions, Twitter revolutions. The content doesn't matter anymore, the problem is the media.

I'm saying this because one of my major points is what went right is also what went wrong. And when we're now trying to see how we can change the situation, when basically we're trying to see what can be done about democracy, we should keep this ambiguity in mind. Because probably some of the things that we love most are going to be also the things that can hurt us most. These days it's very popular to believe that this push for transparency, this kind of a combination between active citizens, new technologies and much more transparency-friendly legislation can restore trust in politics. You believe that when you have these new technologies and people who are ready to use this, it can make it much more difficult for the governments to lie, it's going to be more difficult for them to steal and probably even going to be more difficult for them to kill. This is probably true. But I do believe that we should be also very clear that now when we put the transparency at the center of politics where the message is, "It's transparency, stupid."

Transparency is not about restoring trust in institutions. Transparency is politics' management of mistrust. We are assuming that our societies are going to be based on mistrust. And by the way, mistrust was always very important for democracy. This is why you have checks and balances. This is why basically you have all this creative mistrust between the representatives and those whom they represent. But when politics is only management of mistrust, then -- I'm very glad that "1984" has been mentioned -- now we're going to have "1984" in reverse. It's not going to be the Big Brother watching you, it's going to be we being the Big Brother watching the political class.

But is this the idea of a free society? For example, can you imagine that decent, civic, talented people are going to run for office if they really do believe that politics is also about managing mistrust? Are you not afraid with all these technologies that are going to track down any statement the politicians are going to make on certain issues, are you not afraid that this is going to be a very strong signal to politicians to repeat their positions, even the very wrong positions, because consistency is going to be more important than common sense? And the Americans who are in the room, are you not afraid that your presidents are going to govern on the basis of what they said in the primary elections?

I find this extremely important, because democracy is about people changing their views based on rational arguments and discussions. And we can lose this with the very noble idea to keep people accountable for showing the people that we're not going to tolerate politicians the opportunism in politics. So, for me this is extremely important. And I do believe that when we're discussing politics these days, probably it makes sense to look also at this type of a story.

But also, don't forget, any unveiling is also veiling. [Regardless of] how transparent our governments want to be, they're going to be selectively transparent. In a small country that could be my country, but could be also your country, they took a decision -- it is a real case story -- that all of the governmental decisions, discussions of the council of ministers, were going to be published on the Internet 24 hours after the council discussions took place. And the public was extremely all for it. So I had the opportunity to talk to the prime minister, why he made this decision. He said, "Listen, this is the best way to keep the mouths of my ministers closed. Because it's going to be very difficult for them to dissent knowing that 24 hours after this is going to be on the public space, and this is in a certain way going to be a political crisis."

So, when we talk about transparency, when we talk about openness, I really do believe that what we should keep in mind is that what went right is what went wrong. And this is Goethe, who is neither Bulgarian nor a political scientist, some centuries ago he said, "There is a big shadow where there is much light."

References

1. benedetta berti: conflict and security researcher.

2. Eric Liu: civic evangelist, CEO of citizen university.

3. Gordon Brown: Britain's former prime minister

4. ivan Krastev: In Mistrust We Trust: Can Democracy Survive When We Don't Trust Our Leaders? Amazon, 2013

5. Nick Bostrom: philosopher.

6. paddy ashdown: a former member of the british parliament.

7. parag Khanna: Connectography: Mapping the Future of Global Civilization, amazon, 2016

8. Robert Muggah: megacities expert

9. Robert Muggah: research director of the Igarapé Institute and the SecDev Foundation. Benjamin Barber: a political theorist and the founder of the Global Parliament of Mayors.

10. Shashi Tharoor: India's minister for external affairs.

11. Wanis Kabbaj: TED@UPS